The Ongoing Insurgency in Southern Thailand: Trends in Violence, Counterinsurgency Operations, and the Impact of National Politics

The Ongoing Insurgency in Southern Thailand: Trends in Violence, Counterinsurgency Operations, and the Impact of National Politics

By Zachary Abuza

Institute for National Strategic Studies
Strategic Perspectives, No. 6

Series Editors: C. Nicholas Rostow and Phillip C. Saunders

National Defense University Press
Washington, D.C.
September 2011

First printing, September 2011

For current publications of the Institute for National Strategic Studies, please go to the National Defense University Web site at: www.ndu.edu/inss.

Contents

Executive Summary 1

Introduction 3

Continued Violence: The New Normal 5

Explaining the Changing Levels of Violence 13

Democrat Party Policy Initiatives 17

What Would Change the Equilibrium? 26

Impact of the July 2011 Elections 28

Implications for U.S. Policy 30

Notes 32

About the Author 35

Executive Summary

Since January 2004, a Malay-Muslim–based insurgency has engulfed the three southern-most provinces in Thailand. More than 4,500 people have been killed and over 9,000 wounded, making it the most lethal conflict in Southeast Asia. Now in its 8th year, the insurgency has settled into a low-level stalemate. Violence is down significantly from its mid-2007 peak, but it has been steadily climbing since 2008. On average, 32 people are being killed and 58 wounded every month. Most casualties are from drive-by shootings, but there are also about 12 impro-vised explosive device (IED) attacks a month.

The insurgency is now characterized by less indiscriminate violence and more retaliatory attacks. Insurgents continue to target security forces, government officials, and Muslim mod-erates who seek accommodation with the Thai state as part of efforts to make the region un-governable by limiting provision of social services and driving Buddhists from the south. The overall level of violence may be influenced more by insurgent calculations about the optimum amount of violence needed to advance their political goals than by improved capabilities of the security forces.

Despite better coordination, Thai counterinsurgency operations are still hampered by bu-reaucratic infighting and a lack of professionalism. Human rights abuses by security services with blanket immunity under the Emergency Decree continue to instill mistrust among the local population. Moreover, as long as violence is contained in the deep south, the insurgency will remain a low priority for the new Thai government, which is focused on national political disputes and is reluctant to take on the military by pursuing more conciliatory policies toward the south. Indeed, even under the 30-month tenure of the Democrat Party with an electoral base in the south, the insurgency was a very low priority and its few policy initiatives were insuf-ficient to quell the violence.

The new Pheu Thai government under Prime Minister Yingluck Shinawatra, the younger sister of Thaksin Shinawatra, who was ousted in a September 2006 coup, will have its hands tied in the south. Its election victory and focus on national reconciliation have already engendered mistrust of the Thai military. The new government will be reluctant to criticize the military's handling of the insurgency, take on the culture of impunity, or push for any form of political autonomy. This will make any devolution of political authority unlikely, limiting chances for a negotiated solution. As a result, low level violence is likely to continue indefinitely.

The most important immediate U.S. objective in Thailand is political stability at the na-tional level and deepening bilateral economic ties. Absent a cohesive Thai government with the political will to overcome military resistance to policies that might address underlying causes of the insurgency, U.S. pressure to do more is likely to be ineffective or even counterproductive. Accordingly, the United States should maintain quiet diplomatic pressure on the government to broaden its counterinsurgency efforts and offer any requested intelligence and law enforcement assistance, while being cognizant of Thai sensitivity over its sovereignty.

Introduction

The national elections that took place on July 3, 2011, are unlikely to resolve the intense political polarization that has wracked Thailand since 2006, when Prime Minister Thaksin Shinawatra was ousted in a military coup. Since then, there have been six prime ministers and a series of weak coalition governments that the military has manipulated easily. The elections are also unlikely to lead to any progress in the long-simmering insurgency in the country's three Muslim majority provinces in the deep south. Indeed, the electoral campaign in the Bangkok-centric nation focused on elite politics, the growing rift between the urban middle class and rural constituents, and the future role of the exiled Thaksin. What was glaringly absent was any serious discussion of the insurgency. The two main parties, the incumbent Democrat Party and opposition Pheu Thai Party, both asserted that they would do better at resolving the insurgency than their rival, but neither party outlined any new initiatives or concrete policies.

The Malay-based insurgency in three southern Thai provinces, Yala, Pattani, and Narathiwat, and parts of a fourth, Songkhla, re-erupted in January 2004 and is now in the middle of its 8th year. Roughly 80 percent of the 1.7 million people in these provinces are Muslims and Melayu speakers. The insurgency has claimed the lives of more than 4,500 people and wounded nearly twice that number in some 11,000 incidents of violence and over 2,000 bombings. In the process, the insurgency destroyed much of the social fabric of southern Thailand, particularly in the countryside.[1] Some 20 percent of the minority Buddhist population has abandoned its land, either fleeing the south altogether or moving into the relatively safe towns. The decentralized and madrassa-based insurgency has confounded the Royal Thai Army (RTA) and other security forces, which have been unable to gain the initiative. Despite 60,000 security forces, Thai baht (THB) 145 billion ($4.9 billion) in expenditures, and the arrest of thousands of alleged insurgents, the violence has continued unabated. There are no signs that the insurgency is actually being defeated. The only country with more IED attacks is Afghanistan.

Prime Minister Thaksin Shinawatra was in charge at the start of the insurgency until he was ousted in a September 2006 coup. Thaksin's policies exacerbated the insurgency, which was operating at a very low level in 2004–2005. Thaksin demanded instant results and rotated the leadership of the 4th Army in Southern Thailand at a dizzying rate, with six different commanders in 3 years. The 60,000-strong security forces were disorganized, riddled with corruption, and willing to undermine one another for a greater share of resources. Few troops were deployed, and those who were tended to be in static positions, effectively ceding the countryside to the insurgents. The insurgency gained in strength in 2006–2007, with most government services in the countryside barely intact as the insurgents set about establishing a modest parallel infrastructure.

Following the September 2006 military coup, expectations were high that the junta would tackle the insurgency. Caretaker Prime Minister Surayud Chulanont said all the right things, including making a public apology to the people of the south, mending ties with Malaysia, and promising many reforms. However, little was actually done, furthering popular mistrust of the government. Moreover, the insurgents did not seem to care who was in charge in Bangkok and were unwilling to give the central government a chance. Violence soared in 2007, peaking at an average of more than four people a day being killed by May.

Then, General Anupong Paochinda, commander in chief of the RTA, launched a surge in mid-2007, with a noticeable increase in troops and patrols producing a steady decline in violence in 2008. Following the December 2007 election that restored democratic governance, allies of ousted Prime Minister Thaksin formed a government.[2] But their energies were spent trying to amend the military-drafted constitution and hold onto power. Fearful of another coup, the People's Power Party (PPP) administration gave the army carte blanche in the south. Violence fell, but at the expense of human rights.

In December 2008, the PPP government fell, following pressure and interference by the military and crown. After a decade, the opposition Democrats were out of the electoral wilderness and back in power. The new government of Prime Minister Abhisit Vejjajiva pledged that resolving the situation in the south was one of its top priorities. Hopes were high as the Democrat Party had a strong record on human rights and tended to be less corrupt and abusive than other parties. The south was the Democrats' traditional electoral stronghold,[3] and Democrat Party leaders spoke of a more nuanced approach. However, the new government was quickly confronted by opposition, pro-Thaksin Red Shirt demonstrators who brought policymaking and governance to a standstill, culminating in clashes in May 2010 that left more than 90 people dead. The distracted government paid little attention to the south.

But with the demonstrations crushed in May 2010, a more secure government formed, and national elections anticipated in the first half of 2011, an opportunity existed to address conditions in the south. This opportunity was squandered, as the south remained a low priority for the government and a blot on the prime minister's record. In 30 months in office, he made only four 1-day trips to the south, which is less than a 2-hour flight from Bangkok.

During his tenure and campaign, Prime Minister Abhisit consistently stated that the violence in the south was down, implicitly taking credit for the improved situation. For example, on

February 7, 2011, Abhisit said, "The government is tackling the problem in the right direction. The number of violent incidents has clearly decreased, but it's still not satisfactory because there are still people who get killed." This argument depends on which year is chosen as a baseline. Violence is down considerably from its peak in mid-2007, having ebbed in 2008, before Abhisit was elected. Violence has climbed and remained at a constant level since then. Nonetheless, in an attempt to assert a pre-election victory, Abhisit lifted the Emergency Decree in three districts in the south in late December 2010. Violence in those districts is indeed low, but it always has been. The overall level of violence in the south has not decreased. Indeed, the general secretary of the National Security Council tried to put a positive spin on a deteriorating situation in mid-March: "I concede that the violent unrest is increasing but our officials are determined to work to their utmost ability to resolve the problem. It is difficult to oversee such a wide area. Although fewer incidents occurred, they were more serious."[4] In a trend evident throughout 2011, the number of attacks is down, but their lethality is up.

This paper analyzes the Democrat Party's counterinsurgency (COIN) policies and performance in its 31 months in office, from December 2008 through June 2011. The Abhisit government had the backing of the military, which was in large part responsible for the political machinations that led to the collapse of the previous PPP government in December 2008. Most observers felt the Democrats were better equipped to deal with the south, having deep electoral ties to the region. The paper begins with an analysis of trends in the violence since 2009, looks at the causes of the decline, and then focuses on the policies of the Abhisit government. It continues with an analysis of the impact that the July 2011 elections may have on the conflict and challenges for the Pheu Thai government of Prime Minister designate Yingluck Shinawatra. It concludes with a brief discussion of the insurgency's implications for U.S. policy.

Continued Violence: The New Normal

Violence in every category is down from its peak in mid-2007, though it has held steady since early 2009.[5] More important, the violence has settled into a pattern, with somewhat less indiscriminate violence than at the peak of the insurgency. Victims are targeted more intentionally, with many killings by insurgents in retaliation for abuses or extrajudicial killings by Thai security forces. Many people interviewed in mid-2010 and mid-2011 described the level of violence as "tolerable" and they have little expectation of it diminishing further.

Between December 2008 and June 2011, 949 people were killed and more than 1,700 wounded—a monthly average of 32 and 58, respectively. In 2007, four people a day were being killed, and eight were being wounded (see figure 1).

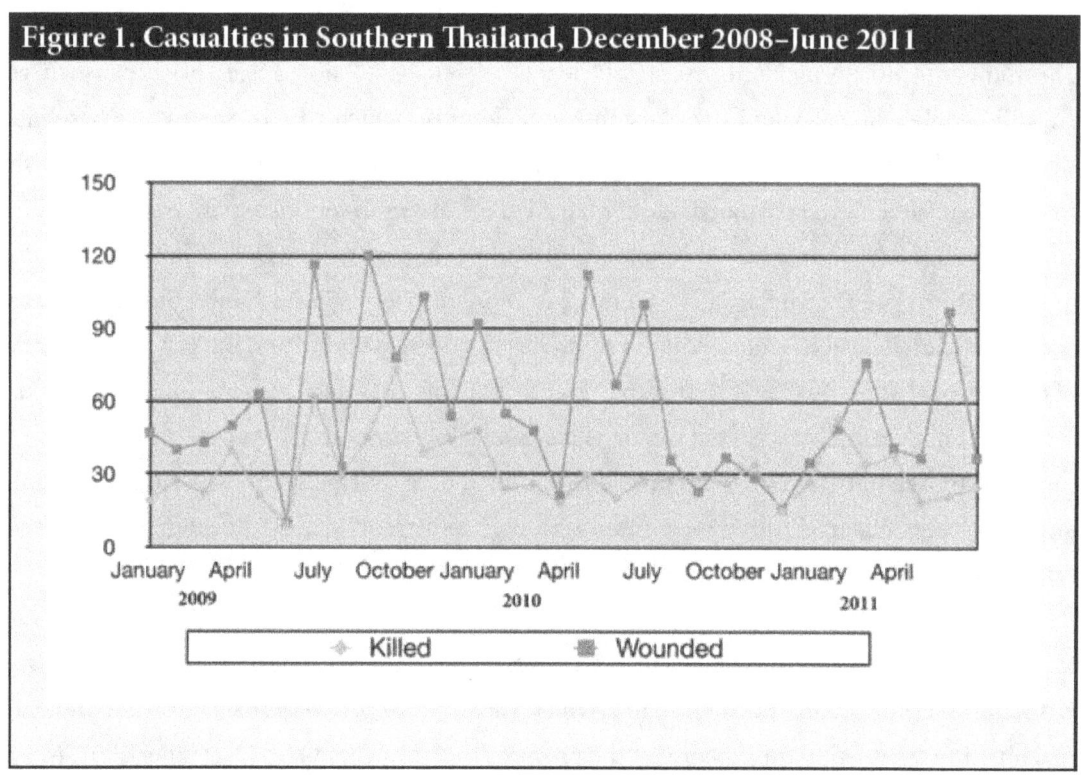

Figure 1. Casualties in Southern Thailand, December 2008–June 2011

Trends in Casualties. As in most insurgencies, security forces represent less than 20 percent of the casualties. Large numbers of soldiers are wounded, but relatively few are killed. Since December 2008, 81 have been killed and 408 wounded (see figures 2 and 3). The decline in deaths is the result of improved force protection, battlefield medicine and clotting kits, larger patrol sizes that deter insurgent attacks, and the equipping of all soldiers in the field with Kevlar vests and helmets. Most of the soldiers who are wounded are victims of IEDs while on teacher protection detail, which takes them to remote villages and is the primary deployment of troops.[6] Nonetheless, they are often deployed on motorcycles, not in armored vehicles.

Police casualties have remained steady. Since January 2009, 44 have been killed and 214 wounded. Police have a small presence in the countryside, with the exception of checkpoints on roads. They usually—but not always—wear Kevlar vests but not helmets. They do not have the same battlefield medical training as soldiers. Police drive thin-skinned pickup trucks, though they have increased the number of trucks that have steel plating.

Taken together, 122 Rangers and Village Defense Volunteers (VDVs) have been killed and 185 wounded. The VDVs are villagers who are lightly armed and wear no helmets or body armor and are very vulnerable to attacks. VDVs often go on teacher protection duty, where

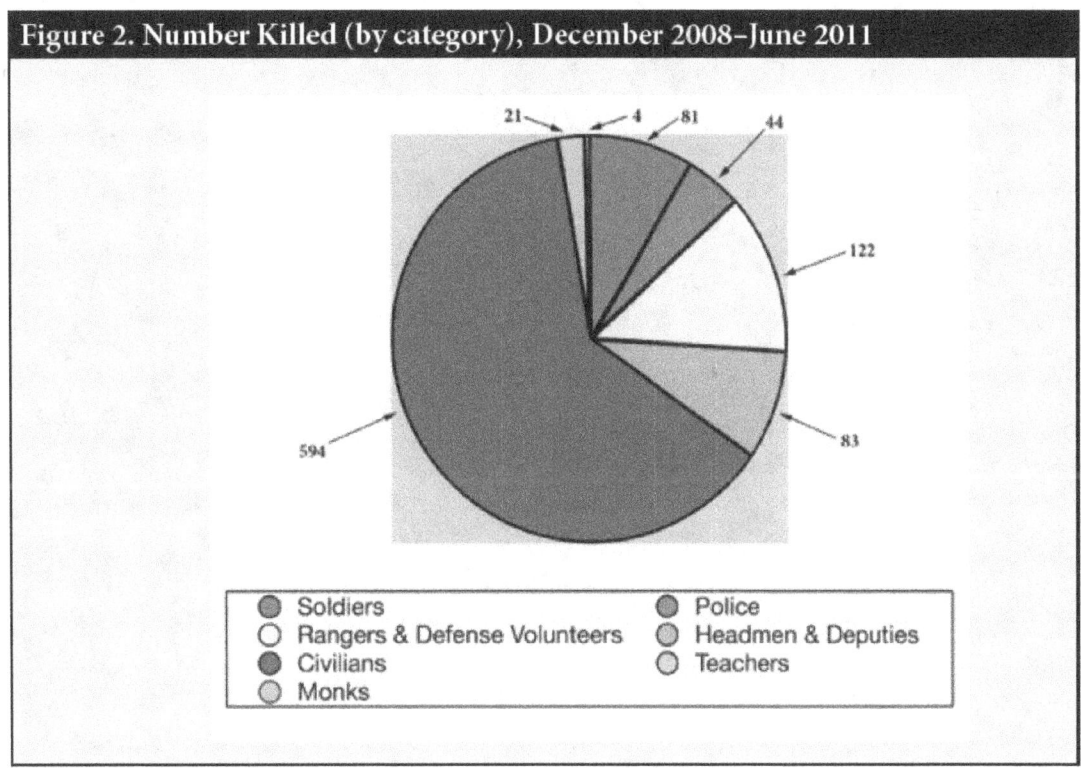

Figure 2. Number Killed (by category), December 2008–June 2011

Legend:
- ● Soldiers
- ○ Rangers & Defense Volunteers
- ● Civilians
- ○ Monks
- ● Police
- ○ Headmen & Deputies
- ○ Teachers

they are sometimes killed or wounded in IED attacks. The number of VDVs is up sharply, with the government having received large shipments of shotguns from Russia—a pilot program of Queen Sirikit subsequently adopted by the government.

The press often refers to the Rangers as "army rangers," although they are poorly trained paramilitaries and not formally part of the army. A disproportionate number of Rangers are migrants from Issarn in northeastern Thailand, and as such tend to have a less nuanced view of the situation in the south and a perceived anti-Muslim bias. They are less restrained in their targeting and have often engaged in extrajudicial killings and other human rights abuses, incurring the wrath of the militants. Their weapons are all decommissioned army guns that often jam or need servicing. They travel loaded into pickup trucks and wear no body armor or helmets, and few have any medical training. Ranger casualties are on the rise, and the government and military alike seem to view them as expendable.

As in most insurgencies, civilians make up the majority of the casualties. Since December 2008, 594 civilians were killed and 902 wounded. In that time, 83 headmen (elected village chiefs) or their deputies have been killed—because they are often in remote locations and die before they can receive medical attention—and fewer than 20 wounded. Headmen remain one

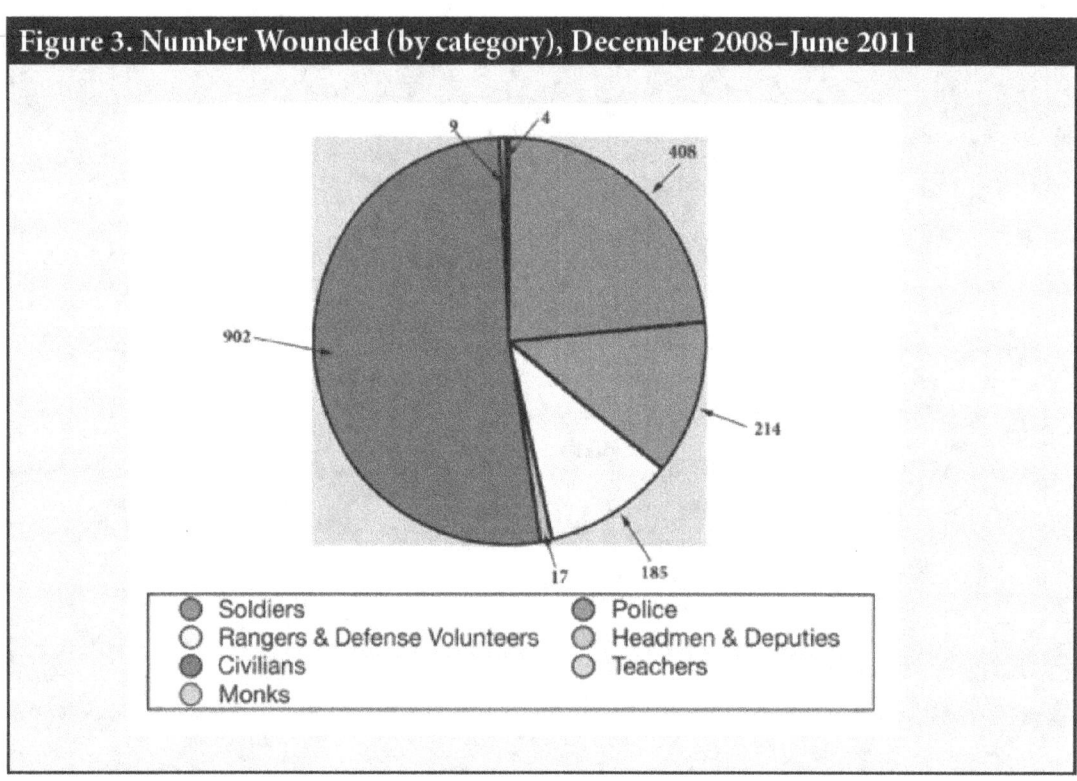

Figure 3. Number Wounded (by category), December 2008–June 2011

Legend:
- Soldiers
- Rangers & Defense Volunteers
- Civilians
- Monks
- Police
- Headmen & Deputies
- Teachers

of the most common targets for insurgents because they are the front line of the Thai state and are perceived as collaborators.

Trends in Types of Attacks. Overall, violence has become less indiscriminate, with insurgent targeting today much more focused and retaliatory in nature. Bombings are down from the peak of 2007 (see figure 4), but there have been 336 bombings between January 2009 and June 2011, an average of just under 12 per month (see figure 5). There have been several large bombings, including nine car bombs and one attempted car bombing. Most IEDs are in the 5- to 10-kilogram (kg) range and are constructed of cooking gas/propane canisters or fire extinguishers filled with ammonium nitrate—that is, things that can be procured easily and often for free.[7] There is a concern that the average size of IEDs may be increasing. For example, of the 12 bombs in May 2011, 3 were between 15 and 20 kgs. Other large car bombings in 2011 include an attack on a police apartment block and one that destroyed 12 shophouses and wounded 18 people.

The only discernible new trend in IEDs is that after years of experimentation, bombs are now routinely detonated by radio devices rather than cell phones. Multiple and simultaneous bombings are down sharply from their peak in 2006–2007, which has done much to

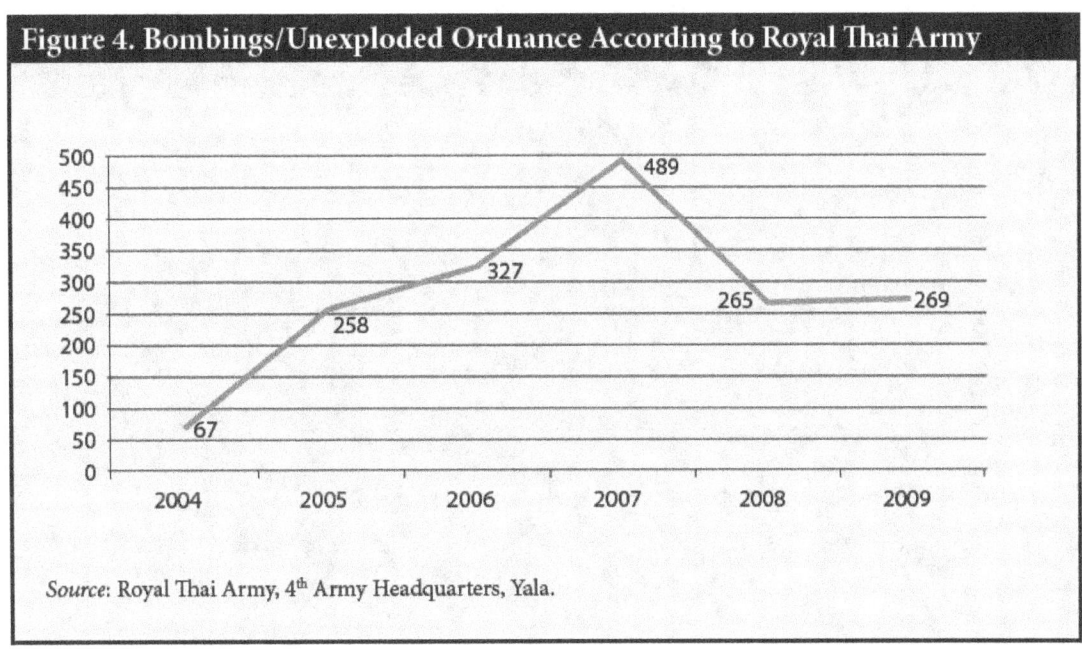

Figure 4. Bombings/Unexploded Ordnance According to Royal Thai Army

Source: Royal Thai Army, 4th Army Headquarters, Yala.

allay concerns that the situation was truly out of the government's control. However, there has been a recent sharp rise in the number of time-delayed IEDs that target first responders. In June 2011, for example, 4 of the 11 IEDs were time-delayed. Overall, there are fewer indiscriminate bombings of soft targets and a greater focus on attacking security forces in remote areas.

Since 2009, there have been significantly more grenade attacks, such as the incident where insurgents lobbed a grenade into a police compound during roll call, killing 2 and wounding 42. Insurgents have used grenades—primarily M–79 grenades—in 58 attacks (see figure 5). Insurgents do not have a regular supply of grenades, and few Thai soldiers are deployed with them, making capture less likely. Yet when insurgents have access to grenades, they use them, as in March 2011, when 13 grenade attacks were mounted.

Shootings, either in roadside ambushes or by motorcycle pillion riders, make up the largest category of killings. The pattern of killings seems far more calculated than it previously was. A pattern of retaliatory attacks has developed, with fewer random killings simply meant to terrorize. Most Muslim-on-Muslim violence has always been about local power struggles, and it still is. Militants have succeeded in driving large numbers of Buddhists out of the countryside, but most of those who remain live in heavily armed Buddhist enclaves. In 2011, three major attacks on rural Buddhist communities have occurred, including an IED attack in a Buddhist village in January 2011 that killed nine, as well as raids in February and March that together killed seven

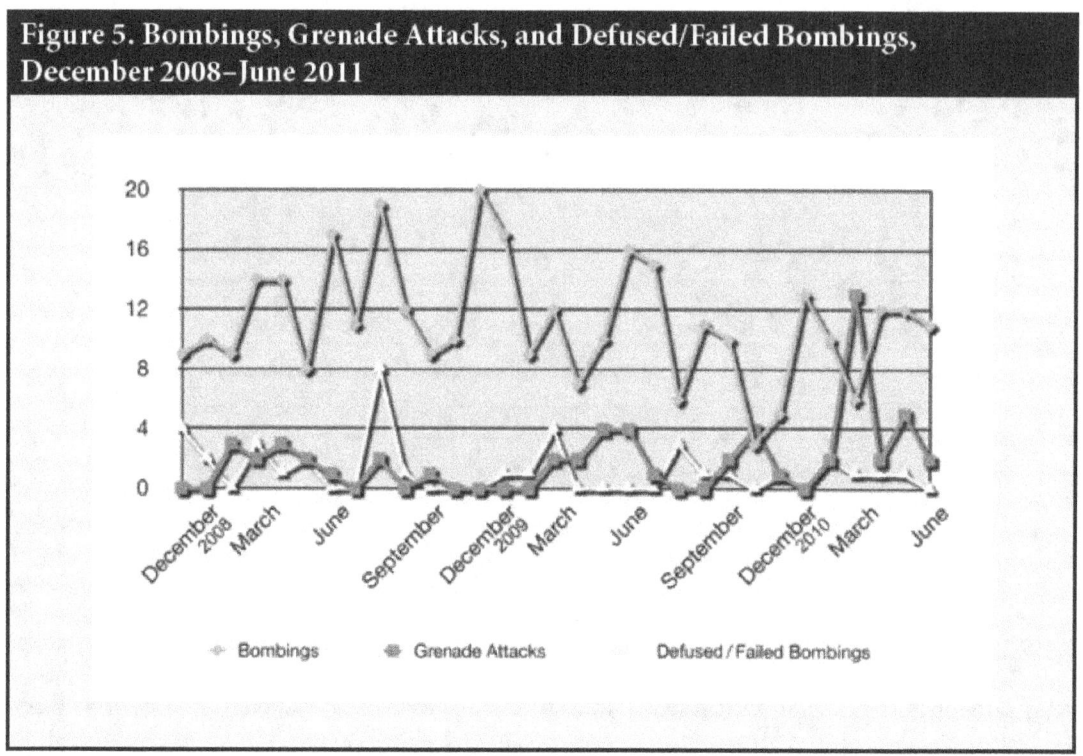

Figure 5. Bombings, Grenade Attacks, and Defused/Failed Bombings, December 2008–June 2011

and wounded seven. Although they tend to be risky for insurgents, attacks on Buddhist enclaves will continue as such deliberate sectarian attacks drive Buddhists out of the area, garner attention in the Bangkok-centric media, and result in vigilante violence. A locally based Muslim journalist argues that there have been a number of gentlemen's agreements involving an end of extrajudicial killings in return for ceasing bombings of soft targets.

Authorities view arson attacks as diversions rather than an end in themselves. Arson attacks on schools are down dramatically; only 12 schools were torched between December 2008 and June 2011. There are several reasons for the decline in attacks. First, there is a permanent military presence at many schools—certainly in the larger towns and along the major highways. Second, many of the old wooden schools have been replaced with concrete structures; there is nothing to torch. And third, there has been a backlash from Muslims who want their children in school, any school. Other arson attacks, such as on government buildings, are also down. Attacks on railroads and cell phone and power transmission lines all declined markedly from their peak in 2007.

There were 11 beheadings between December 2008 and June 2011. Overall, since January 2004, there have been more than 40 beheadings. Militants have desecrated the bodies of 38 victims, which usually entails setting their corpses on fire.

Militants tend to engage in firefights reluctantly and in self defense. Data on firefights is very suspect, as engagements are rarely reported in the press, especially if there are no casualties. Nonetheless, open sources report an average of four prolonged firefights a month. Militants conduct sporadic raids on remote police and army outposts, although some attacks demonstrate high levels of planning and intelligence. The best example of such an attack occurred on January 19, 2011, when insurgents attacked a remote army base, killing 4 soldiers (including their commander) and wounding 13 others. They absconded with at least 20 small arms and assault rifles.

The government is focused on protecting the cities, and in particular the Buddhist population in the south. The countryside has for all intents and purposes been ceded to the militants, particularly at night. People have become inured to the violence, which remains at a tolerable level of about one person killed a day. The flight of Buddhists has stopped, which has always been a priority for the government. Nevertheless, there must be a reason why the rate of killing is not higher. There is obviously some strategic calculation on the part of the militants. The provision of government services, in particular in the education and health sectors, is very low and unlikely to improve due to the tenuous security situation.

Social Costs of the Insurgency. The impact of a long-term, low-level insurgency on a society is always difficult to measure. The social fabric in southern Thailand has clearly broken down, and ethnic and sectarian trust is unlikely to be restored anytime soon. The conflict has had a noticeable impact on the provision of social services.

Two types of victims—teachers and monks—are the most troubling for the government, as attacks on them tend to drive Buddhists out of the south and attract national media scrutiny. The insurgents continue to attack teachers because they are the single most important target in terms of provoking a response from the Buddhist community and the Thai state. Since the insurgency began, more than 140 teachers have been killed. However, only 21 were killed and 9 wounded between December 2008 and June 2011, a sharp decrease. Explanations for the overall decline in teacher casualties vary. On the one hand, the security forces have dramatically increased the size and number of teacher protection patrols. There is also a permanent military presence at many schools—certainly in the larger towns and along the major highways. Teacher protection is the primary responsibility of the military. But the decline also appears to be due to a backlash from the Muslim community. The feeling, as one person told me, is that it is "better to have Siamese schools than no schools at all." In September 2010, a teacher and his wife were gunned down, causing 465 schools across the three provinces to shut down for at least 3 days.

Only four monks have been killed since December 2008, mostly via IED attacks while collecting alms. (Two soldiers were also killed while protecting monks in another incident.) These attacks led the Narathiwat Sangkha Council to ban all alms collection indefinitely, undermining morale of the Buddhist population. Yet the attack had a more pernicious effect when the queen, already a very polarizing figure in the south, took under her patronage two monks wounded in an attack. The queen has been outspoken in her defense of Buddhists in the south and has taken victims under her patronage or paid for funerals of others. This has undermined any pretense of royal neutrality. Authorities think this is significant because previous attacks on monks led to retaliatory attacks on Muslim clerics and teachers, threatening a broader sectarian escalation.

According to government statistics, the majority of those killed between January 2004 and December 2009 were Muslim (2,337 compared to 1,607 Buddhists), though Buddhists were more often wounded—4,207 compared to 2,389 Muslims. What troubles authorities whom I interviewed—all of whom were Buddhists themselves—is that Buddhists make up only 15 percent of the population in the south. Most Buddhists live in large towns; those who have remained in the countryside now live in heavily armed enclaves. One hypothesis about why violence is down is that the insurgents have succeeded in driving out many Buddhists from the south.

The conflict has had a particular impact on women, who account for one-third of the more than 4,500 people killed. The insurgency has produced 2,100 widows and 5,000 orphans since January 2004. But the long-term impact on women and children is even more alarming.

One public health official noted that at present, "Nine out of every 100 women in Pattani, Yala and Narathiwat who gave birth would die"—significantly above the national average, a rate akin to that in Nepal. The number of women dying in childbirth due to pregnancy complications has skyrocketed because widespread violence prevents them from getting proper prenatal care. According to the Southern Border Provinces Administrative Centre, maternal mortality in the south doubled from 2003 to 2006 and is now three times the national standard. Average birth weight is well below the 2.5 kg national average, and infant mortality in the deep south is 30 percent higher than the national average.[8] Children born outside of hospitals are not getting immunizations or having their births registered, making them ineligible for the national healthcare system or public schools. Infant malnutrition rates in the south are also above the national average.

Lack of personnel and daily attacks have forced hospitals to cut outreach services to the bare minimum. In early 2007, the minister of health admitted that half of the estimated 9,000 medical workers in the region had requested transfers out of the area. Replacements are hard to find. In 2007, only 63 percent (29 of 46) of doctors assigned to the deep south took positions there. According to a study by the Public Health Ministry's International Health Policy Programme, only about 1,300 government-employed nurses are working in the five southernmost provinces. In 2007, the government began a THB140 million program to offer 3,000 nursing scholarships to Muslim women, contingent on them working in the south for 3 years. This was a brilliant strategy, as it made the women pillars of the community and stakeholders, providing a challenge for the insurgents who seek to prevent Muslims from working for the Thai state. Interestingly, when the May 2011 class of nursing students graduated and the government upheld its promise and allocated 1,977 civil servant nursing positions for Muslims in the south, there was a backlash from Buddhist nurses and public employee unions.[9] In 2012, the cabinet also assigned 102 graduates in medicine, dentistry, and pharmacology who received government scholarships to positions in the three southern border provinces.

Explaining the Changing Levels of Violence

Violence is down from its 2007 peak, though the level of violence has stayed fairly steady since 2008. Is the decline due to the increased number of Thai security forces, improvements in their capabilities, tactics, and strategy, and the 145 billion baht spent by the government on the south? Or has violence decreased because of a strategic calculation by the insurgents that they have eliminated enough rivals to advance their agenda and a desire not to alienate the Muslim population?

Improvements in the Thai Security Forces: Quantity and Quality? When violence peaked in mid-2007, then–RTA chief General Anupong ordered a "surge" in the south. Today, more than 60,000 security forces are deployed in the three southern provinces, including 30,000 soldiers, 10,000 Rangers, and 20,000 police and other Ministry of Interior and intelligence personnel. During the day, there are visibly more troops on the road. The RTA is trying to strike the right balance between presence and not appearing to occupy the south.

The performance of Thai security forces has improved marginally. Compared to 2007, there are significantly more checkpoints on the highways, with most now run by the army, robustly manned, and including security cameras that record license plates. However, the checkpoints are almost all fixed at the entrances of towns or in front of schools and Buddhist temples. Rolling checkpoints are rare. Troops continue to travel in small groups, either walking along the highways or riding in convoys of two or three motorcycles. They are rarely deployed beyond checkpoints at night. Their primary responsibility is teacher/school protection. The military is only slightly better equipped than it was before the surge; there are still significant shortages of armored vehicles and no helicopters. In short, Thai security forces remain predominantly deployed in static positions.

Although the security forces have not really improved their capabilities or tactics, they deserve credit for a few things. First, they have not overreacted to any event recently and have demonstrated strategic restraint on several occasions. There have been none of the heavy-handed responses that the insurgents seek to provoke. Second, the incompetence demonstrated in 2007, such as an incident when top militants were allowed to slip out of holding cells made of chicken wire, seems to be the stuff of the past. Thai security forces are definitely acting more professional.

Some analysts have bemoaned the RTA's apparent loss of COIN skills. Many cite its past performance in dealing with Muslim insurgents in the south in the 1970s to 1990s, countering the Malayan Communist Party and the Thai Communist Party, and assisting in the secret war in Laos in the early 1960s and in Vietnam. In reality, the RTA became a conventional force despite a security environment centered on low-intensity conflicts and asymmetrical threats. The RTA may have been given too much credit for past COIN successes. The RTA did not defeat the Thai Communist Party, as it often asserts; the movement imploded when China cut off all aid in 1979 as a quid pro quo for Thailand's assistance in rearming the Khmer Rouge. For a well-resourced military that has been the recipient of extensive foreign assistance and training, one may legitimately expect better performance than it has delivered.

Third, the RTA is also taking the threat of Buddhist vigilantism very seriously. One case stands out. In June 2009, a mosque in Narathiwat's Cho-airong District was attacked by a group of gunmen, who killed 11 and wounded 12. Suspicion immediately fell on the RTA, which denied any involvement and argued that the attack was probably the work of militants trying to discredit the RTA and the government. A government spokesman asserted that it was a desperate act of the insurgents. In reality, Buddhist vigilantes perpetrated the attack. The suspects were members of the queen's village volunteer forces and had a lot of high-level supporters. After detaining several of the suspected ringleaders, the RTA was pressured to release them. The RTA then leaked the name and photo of the ringleader, who then killed himself, as did another suspect whose photo was leaked. This sent a strong signal through the community, and since then, Buddhist vigilante attacks have sharply declined. Buddhist vigilantism both undermines the RTA's legitimacy and fuels a cycle of retaliatory violence.[10]

Finally, coordination among the security forces is the best it has been since 2004. In 2002, Prime Minister Thaksin disbanded the Southern Border Provinces Administrative Committee (SBPAC), an Army-led interagency coordinating body established in 1991 that was relatively effective in combating the insurgency. In 2002, Thaksin declared the insurgency defeated and disbanded the agency. Some saw this action as a way to dismantle a key institution that had deep ties to the opposition Democrat Party. Others saw it as a way to shift control over lucrative cross-border smuggling operations from the RTA to the police, to which Thaksin had once belonged.

Interagency cooperation collapsed, and the police dismantled the entire human intelligence network along with the SBPAC's effective dispute resolution mechanism. When the insurgency erupted again in 2004, there was nobody to coordinate military and police responses. Moreover, there is evidence that the RTA allowed the insurgency to fester to discredit the police and wrest back control of the south. The SBPAC was restored following the September 2006 coup. But it had a slow start and was controlled directly by the army's Internal Security Operations Command (ISOC). The agency did not start playing a strong role in coordinating intelligence and tactical operations until late 2009–early 2010.

Nonetheless, turf wars continue to hamper operations. For example, an Australian-funded IED data and mapping center remains controlled by the police, which means that IED attacks on soldiers (who are the targets of the majority of attacks) are not included in the database.[11] The RTA recently requested external funding for its own separate IED data center; to date, however, neither the American nor Australian government has agreed to fund a similar center for the RTA.

In sum, RTA effectiveness has not improved dramatically, but the force is making fewer major mistakes and counterproductive operations, while cracking down on Buddhist vigilantism and improving interagency coordination.

Misguided Priorities. There are still legitimate concerns about how serious the military leadership is about tackling the insurgency. The RTA leadership remains obsessed with elite political machinations in Bangkok, which are unlikely to stabilize anytime soon and will become even more contentious following the death of the ailing 83-year-old monarch, King Bhumibol Adulyadej, and the succession of his son, Crown Prince Maha Vajiralongkorn.

One has only to look at the surge in Thai military spending since the September 2006 coup to see the misguided priorities (see figure 6). In December 2006, the military announced major arms purchases worth $2.3 billion. In 2007, the Minister of Defense requested $9.3 billion for military modernization during the next decade. In September 2008, the RTA announced a second wave of arms purchases worth $191.3 million, followed by a third tranche in January 2009. The vast majority of these planned acquisitions have little to no value in combating an insurgency. They include six Swedish Gripen jet fighters, Chinese surface-to-surface missiles, Russian antiaircraft missiles, and a Singaporean-built amphibious frigate. The only weapons applicable to counterinsurgency operations were six Russian-made Mi-17 helicopters, nearly 100 South African–made armored personnel carriers (APCs), 96 Ukrainian BTR–3 APCs, and Israeli Tavor assault rifles.[12] It is not clear whether any of these weapons will actually be deployed in the south.

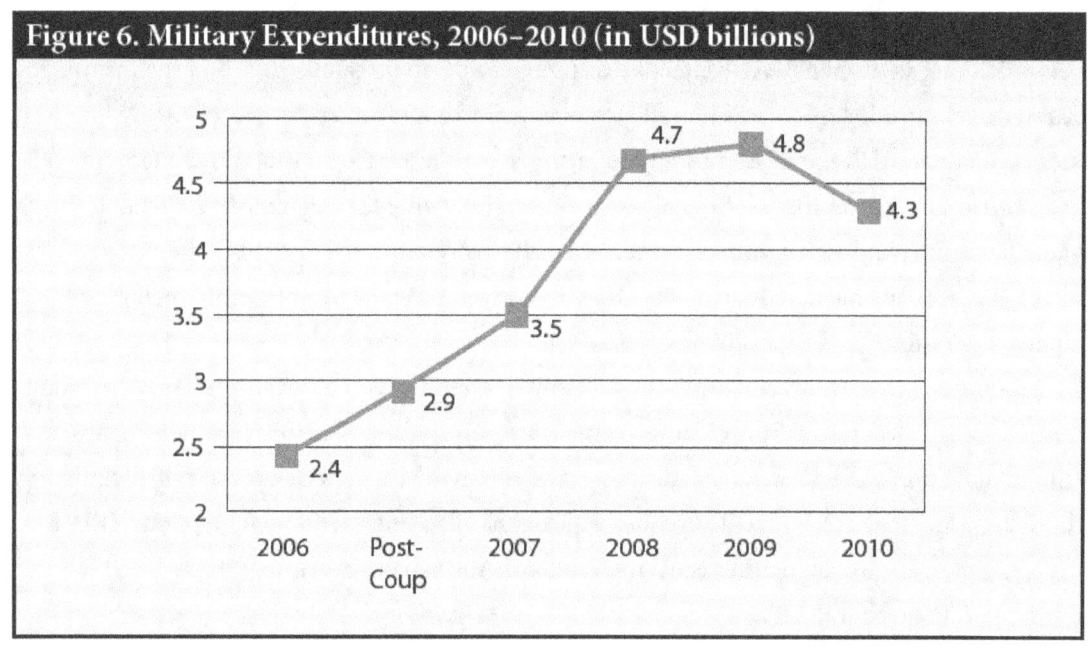

Figure 6. Military Expenditures, 2006–2010 (in USD billions)

In early 2010, as a result of the global economic slowdown, which briefly impacted Thailand, the government asked the military to put purchase of the Ukrainian APCs on hold. The military still received $90.5 million for arms purchases,[13] and with Thailand's economy soaring by late 2010, the RTA has demanded further purchases. The military's shopping list includes more Tavor assault rifles ($60 million), Israeli Negev machineguns, APCs, tanks, surface-to-air missiles, artillery, engineering vehicles, Black Hawk and Cobra helicopters, six used German submarines near the end of their operational life, Seahawk helicopters, and patrol craft. Thailand has a long history of purchasing prestige weapons systems that it neither needs nor can afford. The flagship example is the HTMS *Chakri Narubet*, a Spanish-built aircraft carrier whose Sikorsky helicopters and Harrier jets are grounded due to high operating costs and the lack of spare parts. The Thai military's acquisition program remains focused on prestige systems, not on the equipment needed for its most pressing security threats: the insurgency in the south and low-intensity border skirmishes with Burma and Cambodia.

In terms of resources, the south continues to be a low priority for the government. Abhisit inherited the post-surge 2009 budget of THB27,547 million but cut spending in subsequent budgets (see table 1).

Insurgent Strategic Considerations. The Thai government and military like to take credit for the decline in violence, but there is ample evidence that strategic considerations of the insurgents are also responsible. Insurgent targeting has become more discriminate, with more than half of the

Table 1. Government Budget Allotment for Counterinsurgency Operations in Southern Thailand

Year	Baht (in millions)
2004	13,450
2005	13,674
2006	14,207
2007	17,526
2008	22,988
2009	27,547
2010	16,507
2011	19,102

Source: Isara News Service, "Seven Years Afterward—An Achievement or a Failure?" January 3, 2011.

victims being their coreligionists. The insurgents have set four short- to medium-term goals: to make the region ungovernable; to eliminate political opposition within the Muslim community; to discredit Thai and secular institutions and force people into schools and institutions controlled by the militant network or their allies; and to provoke heavy-handed responses by security forces. The insurgents may have found an equilibrium by using just enough violence to advance their goals without driving the population into the arms of the government or risking a popular backlash. The insurgents claim to have cells in 90 percent of the villages in the south, although nearly all are part-time militants only activated for specific operations. The insurgents are capable of a considerably higher level of attacks but have chosen to limit the level of violence for strategic reasons.

Democrat Party Policy Initiatives

The Abhisit government initiated only a few policies for resolving the conflict in the south, none of which were new, innovative, or bold. All had been attempted to some degree by preceding governments. These measures included some reforms in detention of suspects, negotiations with insurgents, development projects, and bureaucratic reorganization and attempts to civilianize government operations in the south. Overall, the insurgency was a low priority for Abhisit and his government, who made only four 1-day visits to the south since December 2008.

Arrests and Detention of Insurgent Suspects. The number of militants killed and captured since the start of 2009 is down, though this may actually be a positive development. The army began mass detentions of suspects in 2007 and by the end of that year had detained more than 2,000 people. Under the government's Emergency Decree, applied to the five southern provinces since May 2005, suspects could be held without charge for 28 days, after which they had to be either charged or freed. The police often were unable to gather evidence or to persuade potential witnesses to cooperate. Most cases lacked any physical evidence, relying on confessions that defendants and their lawyers claimed were coerced.[14] Of the 7,439 "security cases" identified by the Royal Thai Police, 77 percent remain unsolved. Suspects were identified in only 24 percent of those cases.[15] Only 19 percent of the 7,680 villagers arrested through February 2011 wound up being charged by the police.[16]

The courts have ordered the release of more than 90 percent of detainees. Moreover, 43 percent of the 440 suspects in 238 cases that actually went to trial were acquitted.[17] This has infuriated the army, reducing its already questionable willingness to work with the police and producing more extrajudicial killings. The military got in trouble for holding detainees longer than 28 days by enrolling them in mandatory vocational training programs. Many were later released but not allowed to return to their communities. Many detainees were held 12 to 18 months without ever being charged and, in the absence of double jeopardy in Thai law, were often re-arrested upon release. As one legal defender stated, "The goal is not to find a real culprit, but to hold onto these people for as long as possible."[18]

Indiscriminate arrests and detentions often wind up strengthening the insurgency. If the young men were not insurgents before they were arrested, they sometimes joined the insurgency afterward due to resentment at their treatment by the Thai state or pressure from insurgents who often consider former detainees as government informants.

Between December 2008 and June 2011, the number of arrests dropped significantly. According to open source media reports, which generally underreport, only 76 militants have been killed and 221 captured. Human rights organizations claim that the numbers of arrests and extrajudicial killings are far higher. A few mid-level leaders have been arrested, but relatively few leaders have been detained. Although the Muslim Lawyers Association is handling some 500 cases, many date back to 2007–2008; they admit that the number of cases has gone down.[19]

The military is no longer engaging in broad sweeps that 4th Army officials admit were counterproductive. Thai officials insist that their intelligence has improved. The RTA also asserts that they often know where suspects are but may not have enough evidence to stand up in a court of law.[20] When an incident happens, the military or police have a much more specific idea of who is responsible, making large sweeps unnecessary. The last mass arrest was in October 2009, when police and soldiers raided the Saengtham Wittaya School in Narathiwat's Bacho district, detaining 60 students and religious teachers for questioning; only three had warrants.

There have also been some modest attempts to improve the legal process for detainees and suspects. These include the establishment of national security courts to expedite cases so that suspects do not languish in backlogged civilian criminal courts. The governor of Yala, Kritsada Bunrat, implemented a pilot parole program for detainees held on flimsy charges.[21] Under the program, bail is arranged and suspects are placed under the recognizance of village headmen and religious leaders while awaiting trial. To date, the Thai army and security forces have prevented this pilot program from being implemented across the region.[22]

Despite some calls for it, the military has been able to quash a general amnesty and to impose so many conditions and restrictions on partial amnesties as to render them useless. In an April 2011 meeting with ISOC, religious leaders in Narathiwat made a general amnesty one of their top demands. The RTA used general amnesties extremely effectively in the 1980s and 1990s in dealing with a host of insurgencies throughout the country, although they are extremely unwilling to do so at this time.

Negotiations. Like the Thaksin and Surayud governments, the Abhisit administration participated in some indirect talks with the insurgents. The problem is that not all of the insurgents are on board, and many see little sense in negotiating, believing that the government has nothing tangible to offer.

The leaders of the various Pattani organizations—including Barisan Revolusi Nasional–Coordinasi (BRN–C), Barisan Revolusi Nasional–Kongres (BRN–K), Pattani United Liberation Organization (PULO), Gerakan Mujahideen Islam Pattani (GMIP), and Islamic Liberation Front of Pattani (BIPP)—meet every 2 months in Malaysia.[23] They have been pushed to meet by the Malaysian government, specifically the Malaysian External Intelligence Organization, which reports directly to the prime minister. The Malaysian Ministry of Defense has also played a role in brokering these talks.[24] They have produced no significant results since 2007, when former Malaysian Prime Minister Mahathir Mohamad tried to broker the Langkawi talks. The group most responsible for the violence, the BRN–C, has been reluctant to attend and sees little reason to negotiate. Members have attended the meetings in Malaysia but have not supported talks with the Thai government. The other groups such as PULO, the BRN–K, and BIPP, which are the most vociferous proponents of talks, are seen as pretenders to the cause. Though they played leading roles from the 1970s through the 1990s, they have little to do with the current situation and can neither end nor control the violence. Other than the BRN–C and GMIP, who see no reason to stop fighting, all want to be at the table because their presence conceals the fact that they have little influence. The real problem is generational. If they negotiate, they have to bring the field commanders to the table. As discussed below, the Organization of the Islamic Conference (OIC) is working to unify the groups under the umbrella United Pattani People Council. It is not clear at the time of writing how successful this effort will be.

In March 2011, the Swedish-based Kasturi Mahkota (the self-proclaimed foreign affairs chief of PULO) made the assertion to Singapore's *Straits Times* that PULO forged an alliance with the BRN–C in 2010 and that PULO now acts as the BRN–C's political wing.[25] Yet there is little evidence of this in southern Thailand. The BRN–C has never accepted a role for PULO and has no reason to do so now. The remainder of PULO consists of a few exiles in Malaysia and Europe who command no forces and do not have the loyalty of men on the ground. It is hard to understand what suddenly makes them an attractive ally of the BRN–C.

The active elements of the insurgency consist of roughly 25 to 30 field commanders (*ju-wae*), who have multiple cells reporting to them. The older generation of Malaysia-based leaders has little to offer the field commanders. These leaders do not command or have any financial leverage over them. Finally, the older generation of leaders engaged in talks with the Thai government cannot deliver anything (for example, the Thai government arrested the rest of the mosque massacre suspects). There have also been debates among the different groups over the degree to which Malaysia should be involved. The reality is that Malaysia is a stakeholder, not a neutral broker. With so many militants living and meeting in Malaysia, the Thai government finds it difficult to view Malaysia as impartial.

Part of the problem is the decentralized nature of the insurgency. A number of groups compete for power, and even the most powerful, the BRN–C, lacks any overarching leadership or *amir* (spiritual leader) that everyone respects. Other schisms exist in the Malay community, such as the dispute between the majority Sha'afi sect and the growing community of Wahhabis who are pushing for autonomy.[26] None of the RTA officers, journalists, academics, or human rights advocates interviewed in July 2010 or May 2011 believed that negotiations would bring an end to the violence.

The BRN–C's position that they have no reason to negotiate has some logic. They are not winning, but they are also not losing, which, in an insurgency, is often enough. They are achieving their short-term objectives: they have made the region ungovernable, sown distrust between the citizenry and the state, neutralized moderate political rivals in the Muslim community, and begun to force their constituents away from the secular institutions of the Thai state. Moreover, the BRN–C has legitimate skepticism based on the fact that the Thai government has brought nothing meaningful to the table, such as amnesties, pardons, autonomy, and ending immunity from prosecution for the military and security forces. Despite many promises and policy initiatives since

2004, the government has failed to implement any durable reforms on issues such as language and education. The Abhisit government, beholden both to the crown and to the military, cannot even begin negotiations on autonomy for the south. In November 2009, Abhisit stated that autonomy would not resolve the issue: "I am confident that fairness is the best way to resolve the conflict [there]." RTA commander in chief General Prayuth Chan-ocha was even more explicit: "No matter what, the three provinces cannot be separated or given even self-rule because that would be against the constitution."[27]

Development Funds. One Abhisit government initiative was to massively increase the amount of funding for development projects. The Abhisit government spent THB109 billion on security and development in the south between 2004 and 2008 and earmarked THB63 billion for the "Development Plan for the Special Area—5 Southern Border Provinces" for fiscal years 2009–2012.[28] This is an enormous investment, but it may not have the desired effects.

The insurgency in the south has never been about poverty. According to the United Nations Development Programme's (UNDP's) most recent report on Thailand,[29] the Muslim deep south lags in some areas but is near the top of national rankings in others, such as health and housing. In terms of total Human Achievement Index (HAI) rankings,[30] the picture in the south is very mixed (see table 2). Songkhla is ranked 4th of 76 provinces, Yala 32d, while Narathiwat and Pattani are in the lower half, ranked 65th and 69th, respectively. By almost every measure, the provinces in Issarn, in northeast Thailand, are the poorest and least developed. Investments of development resources would do better in the north, where they might help ameliorate the social tensions in Thailand caused by the 2009–2010 street demonstrations between the Red Shirts and the government.

Data on income is more complicated. In terms of household income, three of the four southern provinces are well in the top half of the nation: Songkhla (14th), Yala (19th), and Narathiwat (36th). Only Pattani (54th) is in the bottom half. While the incidence of poverty in Pattani (19.7 percent) and Narathiwat (20.2 percent) is high (more than twice the national average), the rates in Yala and Songkhla are very low (see figure 7). In terms of employment, the south is faring poorly; the HAI composite scores of all four provinces are in the lower half. But if one looks more closely at the actual employment and underemployment figures, the south is not doing worse than most regions. What is of greater concern is income inequality in the deep south. The Gini coefficients—a quantitative metric that shows income inequality—of all four provinces are well below the national average, and Yala is one of the most inequitable provinces in the country. But to be fair, the UNDP sounds the alarm for inequality across Thailand, which it terms a "persistent" problem and a "worsening trend."[31]

Table 2. Human Achievement Index Rankings of Deep South Provinces (ranking out of 76 provinces)

	Pattani	Yala	Narathiwat	Songkhla
Health	24	5	14	3
Education	71	43	75	5
Employment	59	74	47	43
Income	54	19	36	14
Housing	38	6	21	8
Family	74	73	75	59
Transportation	58	30	71	7
Political Participation	62	58	60	41
Total HAI Ranking	69	32	65	4

Source: United Nations Development Programme.

The problem may be exacerbated rather than solved by THB63 billion in development funding. The real questions are who will spend those funds and how they will be spent. As it stands, the military's ISOC will be responsible for the disbursement of most funds. The Southern Border Provinces Administrative Centre only administers a handful of projects for education and reconciliation. The Abhisit government said it wanted a softer, development-oriented approach, but that policy was administered by the same security institution whose role the government sought to reduce.

There is also a legitimate concern over whom the funds will benefit. If funds are misappropriated—always a possibility in a country with high rates of corruption—or directed primarily to Buddhists or Muslims who have openly sided with the government, the effort will further alienate the population. Since 2004, the government has gone out of its way to use fiscal means to punish "red zones"—villages with high rates of insurgent activity—which is hardly an effective counterinsurgency program. The government has suggested that it will continue to reward regions with lower rates of unrest. One nongovernmental organization (NGO) leader estimated that roughly 20 percent of the 2009 development funds for the south simply vanished.[32] The government is bracing for a similar amount in the 4-year budget. The NGO official said that government auditors were afraid to be deployed to the south—and not because of the insurgency. More cynically, many have suggested that the funds were being used to shore up the

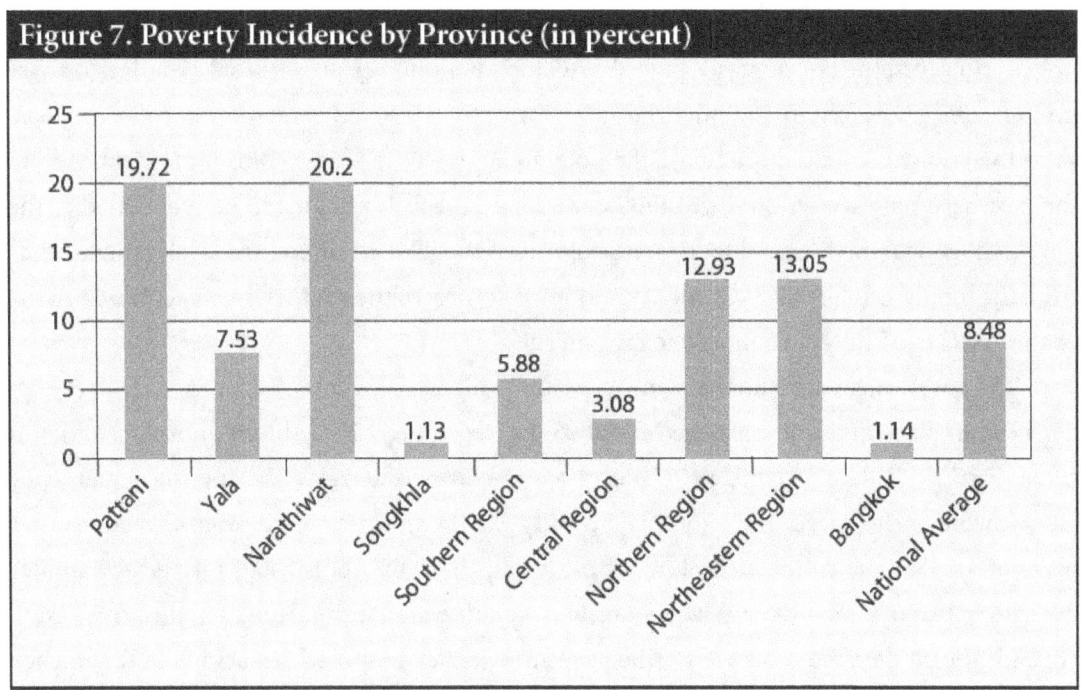

Figure 7. Poverty Incidence by Province (in percent)

Democrat Party's support base in the Buddhist-majority upper south in the hopes of improving its performance in the May 2011 elections.

The one area where UNDP data shows the southern provinces really lagging is in education. This is partly due to insurgent efforts to kill and intimidate teachers, burn schools, and undermine the secular educational system. But the problem has deeper roots. In mid-2011, the education ministry allocated a budget of THB110 million to improve education in the deep south and halt the flood of students who drop out by the end of middle school, estimated to be more than 40,000 in the past few years.[33]

Ultimately, government spending can only do so much. At some point, the private sector will have to step in and invest to create jobs and sustainable economic growth. Since 2004, investment has flooded out of the region. In 2009, Narathiwat and Pattani registered no private investment projects, while Yala had only one worth $2.1 million.[34] Without security, investment and economic growth will remain limited.

Strengthening Civilian Control. One of the Abhisit government's priorities was to return the Southern Border Provinces Administrative Committee to civilian rule, which was accomplished in an April 2011 law. Since its reestablishment in late 2006, the SBPAC had been under direct control of the Army's ISOC. Under the new law, the SBPAC operates independently, and its leadership is appointed directly by and reports to the prime minister. In theory, the SBPAC secretary-general will be able to discipline, and even dismiss, high-ranking officials including police. However, the law does not give SBPAC jurisdiction over prosecutors or judges or over military officers, who remain under the authority of the ISOC.[35] In the months following passage, the government did little to use the body to empower moderate Muslim leaders, who in the past have only served on the SBPAC's advisory panel.[36] It remains to be seen whether the new civilian agency will be able to wrest control of the THB63 billion in development funds from the military. While SBPAC will have nominal control of the south, few expect the 4th Army or the ISOC to be fully accountable to civilian rule.

The government announced plans to partially lift the draconian Emergency Decree that has been in place in the south since May 2005. In December 2010, Abhisit announced that in three districts, Pattani's Mae Larn, Narathiwat's Sukhirin, and Yala's Kabang, the Emergency Decree would be replaced by the Internal Security Act (ISA), which has been instituted in other parts of Thailand since the Red Shirt unrest began in 2009. Abhisit had pushed for similar changes in two other districts: Yala's Betong and Narathiwat's Waeng. However, the army resisted, and Abhisit deferred to its views. The government later proposed replacing the Emergency Decree with the ISA in four districts of Songkhla, but that proposal was not acted on.

The government contends that the ISA allows security forces to retain some additional powers, such as the ability to detain people without charge for 7 days, while including some—albeit very weak—amnesty provisions that will promote reconciliation. Cynics saw this as a politically motivated policy, implemented to demonstrate security improvements before fiercely contested national elections. Others point to the fact that the ISA is draconian in its own right and has fundamentally eroded human and civil rights across the country since its passage. For them, the shift is just window dressing.[37] Lifting of the Emergency Decree has played well in the media, but it does not indicate a measurable improvement of the situation. Violence, never high in those three districts, has fallen. But elsewhere, the rates of violence remain persistent.

Are the Reforms Enough? These reforms and initiatives were not bad policies, but they were insufficient to resolve the conflict. Even if welcomed by the local Malay community, they were seen as too little, too late. The government did not push for the reforms that could make a real difference and start to win the hearts and minds of the population: tackling the issues of security force immunity, legal reforms and the protection of defendant rights, and serious discussions about political autonomy. Such reforms would require the government to take on and overcome opposition from the military and security forces. However, the south was a low priority for the Democrat government, which was obsessed by the political threat posed by the

Red Shirts and Thaksin's allies and unwilling to challenge the authority of the military, whom many saw to be the Democrats' patrons.

Allegations of torture by security forces persist. To date, more than 1,000 complaints have been brought before the national Human Rights Commission, with little result. Photographs documenting torture are admissible in court but carry little weight in judicial deliberations. The testimony of doctors is weighted highly, but Muslim lawyers complain that doctors are not allowed to examine suspects in a timely manner. Lawyers also argue that the Thai security forces have employed other coercive methods that make allegations of torture harder to prove.[38]

With the Emergency Decree and Internal Security Act in place, the security forces enjoy nearly full immunity for their actions, something that has alienated the Muslim community. Surayud Chulanont's 2006–2007 interim government—installed following the September 2006 coup—pledged to tackle the issue of security force impunity, as did Abhisit's government. Yet the Abhisit administration proved unwilling to take on the issue, an enormous disappointment for many who had high expectations that he would address the problem. Indeed, when I interviewed him in July 2010, he seemed oblivious to the continuing human rights abuses. In the past 2 years, several major legal cases against security forces have been dropped, while a number of accused officers have been acquitted, fueling resentment amongst the local population. For example, on March 11, 2011, a court of appeals acquitted police major Ngern Thongsuk, who had been convicted in criminal court in 2006 for his role in the 2004 disappearance of Muslim human rights lawyer Somchai Neelaphaijit. He had been sentenced to 3 years in jail, but the appeals court found insufficient evidence. This was already a very sensitive issue. In the original 2006 trial, four other police defendants were acquitted due to insufficient evidence, infuriating the Muslim community. Not a single officer has been convicted of human rights abuses. Indeed, all those accused in egregious incidents such as the Krue Se mosque raid and the Tak Bai incident have been acquitted.

On March 21, 2011, Army chief General Prayuth Chan-ocha publicly apologized for the Krue Se and Tak Bai incidents: "The two incidents should not have happened. I apologize to all southerners, especially relatives of the dead, even though at the time I was not yet in this position. The incidents happened because of carelessness on the part of the authorities. I promise not to let anything like that happen again." Nevertheless, the RTA worked assiduously to exonerate all involved.[39] The negative impact was compounded by General Prayuth's call for enhanced authorities for government forces, whom he said were at a disadvantage against guerrillas. Muslims in the south repeatedly warned me that until the issue of social justice is tackled, the insurgency cannot be quelled.

A test of the government's commitment to deal with the culture of security force impunity will be the upcoming trial in the Pattani provincial court of those accused of the death of a detained suspected insurgent, Sulaiman Naesa, who was found hanging in his cell at the Ing-khayutborihan military camp May 30, 2010, after being detained without charge 8 days prior. The military claimed that the suspect took his own life, but his family alleges that his body had visible signs of torture and that the government was responsible for his death. Despite the trial date, few Muslims see any reason for optimism. Muslims in the south repeatedly warned me that until the issue of social justice is tackled, the insurgency cannot be quelled.

What Would Change the Equilibrium?

Although the Thai government increased resources, manpower, and funding for dealing with the insurgency, it currently remains a low priority for the Thai political and military elite. The fact that the government and RTA officially label militants as "perpetrators of violence" rather than "insurgents" says a lot about the government's own naiveté. It has neither the political will, nor the strategy, nor the tactics to defeat the insurgents decisively and negotiate from a position of strength. Bangkok cannot solve the south's problems until it solves its own problems, a situation that looks a long way off. No one in the Thai polity is willing to implement the necessary decentralization and autonomy that might appease the insurgents, even though Anand Panyarachun's Blue Panel Commission on National Reconciliation's recommendations to that effect are now on the table. At the same time, without external assistance, a broader base of popular support, and a program that goes beyond the nihilist violence of making the region ungovernable and driving out Buddhist Thais, the insurgents can never win. Although they could increase the level of violence, the insurgents lack the resources or capability to escalate the conflict dramatically. Indeed, they benefit politically from a continuing calibrated low level of violence. The result is a stalemate that is likely to continue indefinitely. What might change the current equilibrium? There are three plausible scenarios, though none seems very probable.

First, a surge in external support could allow the insurgents to escalate the conflict. This appears unlikely, since the insurgents currently receive no state-sponsored support, and sub-state support is limited. Malaysia might enjoy watching the Thais flail around in the south, and it provides political fodder in the Malaysian parliament. However, at the end of the day, Kuala Lumpur's relationship with Bangkok is too important to provide support to the Thai insurgency. Bilateral trade is growing,[40] and these founding members of the Association of Southeast Asian Nations need each other diplomatically. Thailand has worked assiduously to improve ties with

Malaysia since the interim government of Surayud Chulanont, though many things still irk Kuala Lumpur. Does Malaysia benefit from 20-kilogram IEDs being detonated less than 200 miles north of its capital? If the Thai authorities are correct that the insurgents are funding themselves through the sale of illegal narcotics, Malaysia has even more to lose by tacitly supporting the insurgency.

No one else in the region would gain from supporting the insurgents. Individuals and especially militant groups in Indonesia have paid their coreligionists in southern Thailand lip service, but given only limited material support. The Indonesian-based terrorist group Jemaah Islamiyah (JI) has broken down into smaller groups, raising the possibility that individual JI members could flee to southern Thailand to escape Indonesian police dragnets. But the Thai insurgents do not need JI members for technical support. The Moro Islamic Liberation Front in the Philippines is too weak and too preoccupied to offer significant training or assistance. There is always a concern in the post–bin Laden world that al Qaeda will spin out additional franchise groups. But so far, the evidence suggests that Malay insurgents are only going to al Qaeda Web sites for technical manuals on bombmaking and other propaganda. The one possibility would be if Lashkar-e-Taiba steps into the void. However, a significant infusion of external support is unlikely.

Second, the Thai government (and the military in particular) is very concerned that the insurgents are trying to internationalize the conflict. Thai officials repeatedly point to OIC interference and assert that the militants are trying to use the OIC to internationalize the situation. Clearly, the OIC has become more important now that Malaysia no longer holds the rotating chair, and the organization is poised to issue a report critical of Thailand.[41] More important, the OIC has been working to link the various insurgent groups into a unified grouping, the proposed United Pattani People Council, which would be represented in the OIC. While significant, the OIC's involvement may not be enough. For one thing, many militants mistrust the OIC, which gave Thailand observer status in 1997. Militants tried to bomb a delegation led by the OIC secretary-general in May 2006 because they thought that the grouping was whitewashing the Thai government's handling of the south. Nonetheless, even a more concerted OIC effort is unlikely to compel the factions to operate on a more unified basis and coalesce around a common negotiating position. The BRN–C really has neither a reason to share power with the other groups, nor an overwhelming reason to negotiate.

Third, Thai security forces could get lucky and neutralize a critical mass of insurgents. In May 2011, they killed a senior militant commander, arguably one of the most important counterinsurgency successes in years. If they could build on this operation with aggressive follow-up operations, they might significantly degrade the insurgency. A much more effective COIN effort could potentially compel the insurgents to negotiate or to leave the south and begin a terrorist campaign targeting Bangkok and tourist venues such as Phuket. While a terrorist campaign outside the south could cripple Thailand's critical tourist industry, it would galvanize public support behind intensified counterinsurgent operations. However, such an improvement in the operational effectiveness of the military and security appears unlikely. The resolution of the situation in the south remains a low priority for the military, which is more concerned with elite politics in Bangkok and sees the south as a mere justification for increased budgets.

In short, the current low-level insurgency that the government and military are not committed to defeating—and that the insurgents are unwilling to escalate—will continue at a slow boil.

Impact of the July 2011 Elections

During the electoral campaign, the south was a minor issue for the two major parties. The Democrats were confident of dominating the local seats and party lists, as the south has been one of their two electoral strongholds (the other being Bangkok). In the run-up to the election, opinion polls indicate that the Thai public saw the Democrats as better able to resolve the insurgency. The Democrats predicted that they would win at least 9 of the 11 seats in the 3 southern provinces, despite winning only 5 seats in 2007.

Yingluck Shinawatra, the new Pheu Thai leader and younger sister of Thaksin Shinawatra, made one prominent and well-received campaign swing in the south in mid-June. She offered a few policy initiatives, including greater public input into decisionmaking, increases in the number of Muslims who could go on the annual Hajj pilgrimage to Mecca, and establishment of a "special administrative zone in the three southernmost border provinces." However, she was very short on specifics.

Five other parties campaigned in the south: Bhum Jai Thai, Thaen Khum Phaendin, Prachatham, Chart Thai Pattana, and Matubhum, but only Matubhum made the south the cornerstone of its campaign. Matubhum was established by and serves as the political vehicle of former RTA chief and 2006 coup leader General Sonthi Boonyaratglin. The party hoped to increase its total number of seats from 3 to 10 by focusing its campaign in the Muslim-majority southern provinces whose residents may be disaffected with the two mainstream parties. Matubhum's campaign claims of better policies toward the south were a stretch: violence surged during the coup period, and Sonthi gave the military carte blanche to deal with the violence.

Though Sonthi is a Muslim himself, he is from the north and not an ethnic Malay, and is also suspect in the eyes of many southerners for his obeisance to the monarchy.

The election results in the south were not a surprise. Although the opposition Pheu Thai won an outright majority at the national level, 265 seats out of 500, compared to the Democrats' 159 seats (the remainder going to 9 other parties),[42] Pheu Thai did not win a single seat in the deep south. The Democrat Party won 9 of 11 seats, with Matubhum and Bhum Jai Thai winning one each. It was a stinging rebuke for Pheu Thai and its leader, Yingluck Shinawatra, and does not bode well for her government in developing new policies or garnering broad public support. She will lead a 6-party coalition government, giving her an ample majority—more than 300 seats—but she will not have an easy time in formulating any new policies in the south.

Nor will the prime minister have an easy time with the RTA leadership, who were outspokenly pro-Democrat during the campaign. General Chan-ocha even warned the general public in a televised speech not to vote for "bad people," a thinly veiled reference to Pheu Thai. The reality is that the RTA designed the 2007 constitution to prevent a powerful political party from emerging—which is exactly what happened. The military prefers a system based on weak coalitions that can be manipulated to protect its interests. Pheu Thai's dominance at the polls is a clear repudiation of the RTA's political meddling since the September 2006 coup. While the RTA leadership has pledged to respect the election results, it does not mean that they will make life easy for Yingluck. This will be even more the case if she uses her majority to push through a parliamentary amnesty for her brother, allowing him to return from exile. She has made "national reconciliation" her top priority, which in the RTA's eyes is a code word for returning her brother to the country and releasing jailed Red Shirt activists. In terms of policies, she is unlikely to distance herself from her brother, and that too will infuriate the RTA leadership.

Like the PPP government of Samak Sundaravej that ruled from February to December 2008, Prime Minister Yingluck has to be constantly concerned that the military, while "respecting" electoral results, will put pressure on the coalition partners and individual Pheu Thai members of parliament to defect to the opposition. While this will be harder to accomplish as Pheu Thai itself won an absolute majority, the defection of coalition members will make governing a greater challenge for Pheu Thai.

Similarly, her government will be unable and unwilling to challenge the military in its handling of the south, which will remain a very low priority. Despite her campaign pledge for a special administrative zone in the south that has significant local backing, Prime Minister

Yingluck is astute enough to know that any form of autonomy for the three provinces is an absolute nonstarter for the military and will therefore go unpursued.[43] She is very unlikely to call on the military to hold itself accountable for abuses in the south, or push to lift the Emergency Decree or ISA or amend the laws that give security forces blanket immunity.

There are a few things Yingluck can do. She should not follow her brother's lead. Thaksin Shinawatra punished regions that did not vote for his party by starving them of development funds. Yingluck should maintain the moral high ground and continue to support the Democrat government's attempt to civilianize SBPAC and its control over development projects. She can also push for some limited legal reforms regarding detainees. But these are very small steps.

Implications for U.S. Policy

The insurgency in southern Thailand is a low-level concern for U.S. policymakers and security planners. Despite past concern over Thailand's handling of the insurgency, fears have dissipated since violence declined after 2007. So long as the violence has remained contained in the deep south and no U.S. citizens or interests have been targeted, the United States has maintained a quiet public position.

U.S. officials likely fear that too much public criticism will further damage ties with the RTA, which have been strained since the September 2006 coup. The United States has no interest in permanent military bases in Thailand, but access to U-tapao Royal Thai Navy Air Base as a forward operating base, especially for humanitarian assistance and disaster relief, is extremely useful. Likewise, the Department of Defense places priority on the annual Cobra Gold training exercise in Thailand, the largest multilateral military exercise in the Asia-Pacific. There are also concerns about China's deepening security ties to Thailand. In October 2010, China and Thailand held their first bilateral military exercises, accompanied by a media blitz.

The United States does share some intelligence and provide some COIN training to Thailand.[44] But such security cooperation is very low key and not in either country's interest to publicize. U.S. law enforcement and intelligence ties with Thailand remain deep, and bilateral cooperation in the past few years has led to the interception of a large cache of arms from North Korea in mid-2010, the capture of high-value terrorist suspects, and the arrest and December 2010 extradition of alleged arms smuggler Viktor Bout.

The Obama administration has raised the profile of Southeast Asia in U.S. policy, with President Barack Obama making two trips to the region, Secretary of Defense Robert Gates making three, and Secretary of State Hillary Clinton making two since January 2009. The administration's policy toward the region is more holistic and less singularly focused on counter-terrorism and COIN. Such a policy better addresses the range of U.S. interests in the region, but the reality is that a significant amount of ungoverned space continues to exist in the heart of insular Southeast Asia.

The most important immediate U.S. objective in Thailand is political stability at the national level and deepening bilateral economic ties. Absent a cohesive Thai government with the political will to overcome military resistance to policies that might address underlying causes of the insurgency, U.S. pressure to do more is likely to be ineffective or even counter-productive. Accordingly, the United States should maintain quiet diplomatic pressure on the government to continue its counterinsurgency efforts and offer any requested intelligence and law enforcement assistance, while being cognizant of Thai sensitivity over its sovereignty. The U.S. military should also continue low-level COIN training and exercises and training missions in areas such as battlefield medicine. This course of action should allow the Thai government to keep violence in the south in check, but it is unlikely to resolve the ongoing conflict. And under the current political climate, any move to decentralize authority is untenable. Such a resolution probably will have to await some degree of national political reconciliation that allows Thai civilian leaders to devote more attention and political creativity to solving the insurgency.

Notes

[1] For more on the insurgency through 2006, see Zachary Abuza, *Conspiracy of Silence: The Insurgency in Southern Thailand* (Washington, DC: United States Institute of Peace, 2009).

[2] Thaksin's Thai Rak Thai party was legally banned in May 2007. It was replaced by the People's Power Party, which in turn was banned in December 2008 and replaced by the Pheu Thai Party.

[3] While the media and pundits often cite the fact that the south is the Democrats' stronghold, this is debatable. The Democrats dominate the Buddhist-majority provinces of the upper south, but their hold on the Malay-majority provinces has eroded. After winning 11 of the region's 12 seats in the 2005 election, the Democrats won only 5 in the 2007 poll.

[4] Thai News Agency, "Insurgency in Thailand's South Declining in Momentum," March 20, 2011.

[5] My data are based on open source reporting and as such are lower than official figures. Not all casualties are reported in the media, and many who are reported as wounded later die. I indicate when I use official data. I do not have access to official data on a regular basis, and when I do, it tends to be aggregate numbers. By carefully coding open source data, I am able to do much more detailed statistical analysis on victim types, location of attacks, trends in how people were killed, size of improvised explosive devices, and so forth.

[6] Nearly half the soldiers deployed in the south are assigned to teacher protection details, and at the close of the school day, there are visibly more soldiers deployed.

[7] There have been a number of motorcycle bombs in markets; authorities are trying to thwart these attacks by asking people to raise their motorcycle seats when they park. People resist this because it is the "storage" on a motorcycle, but I did see a handful of markets in Narathiwat where this was required.

[8] Sanitsuda Ekachai, "Silent Deaths in Restive South," *Bangkok Post*, February 17, 2011, available at <www.bangkokpost.com/opinion/opinion/222013/silent-deaths-in-restive-south>.

[9] Author interview, Bangkok, May 15, 2011.

[10] Author interview with a Thai journalist, Yala, July 3, 2010.

[11] Author interview with an Australian diplomat, Bangkok, July 6, 2010.

[12] "Cabinet Nod for B7.7bn to Buy Arms, Equipment," *Bangkok Post*, September 26, 2007; Patrick Winn, "Thailand Plans $191.3M Arms Purchase," *Defense News*, September 12, 2008; and Patrick Winn, "Muslim Insurgency Triggers Thai Military Spending Blitz: Military Shores Up Attack Helicopters, APCs and Assault Rifles," *Defense News*, February 2009.

[13] The government also delayed the purchase of six additional Gripen jet fighters. Brian McCartan, "Thai Military Puts Up Spending Defense," *Asia Times*, February 26, 2010.

[14] Author interview with a team from the Muslim Lawyers Association, Bangkok, July 10, 2010. Anyone arrested or detained under national security laws must sign a confession of sorts before being released.

[15] Isara News Service, "Seven Years Afterward—An Achievement or a Failure?" January 3, 2011.

[16] Sanitsuda.

[17] Muslim Lawyers Association interview; "Seven Years Afterward."

[18] Muslim Lawyers Association interview.

[19] Ibid.

[20] Author interview with RTA intelligence officers, Bangkok, May 19, 2011.

[21] Thai journalist interview, Yala.

[22] Author interview with a Thai journalist, Washington, DC, November 17, 2010.

[23] Thai media routinely label the insurgents Runda Kumpulan Kecil (RKK)—literally small group training that was thought to have originated in Indonesia. The RKK is not an organization.

[24] Author interview, Washington, DC, May 27, 2010.

[25] Nirmal Ghosh, "Talks on Thai South to Resume, Meeting Involving Separatist Leaders to Take Place Outside Thailand," *The Straits Times*, March 4, 2011.

[26] Thai journalist interview, Yala.

[27] "Army Chief Apologises to Southerners," *Bangkok Post*, March 23, 2011, available at <www.bangkokpost.com/news/security/228221/prayuth-apologises-to-southerners>.

[28] United Nations Development Programme (UNDP), *2009 Thailand Human Development Report* (UNDP: Bangkok, May 2010), 45.

[29] Ibid.

[30] The Human Achievement Index is 8 indices based on 40 indicators. See ibid., 101–102.

[31] Ibid., 79–80.

[32] Author interview, Bangkok, July 8, 2010.

[33] "B110 million Earmarked for Deep South Schools," *Bangkok Post*, May 27, 2011.

[34] In comparison, in 2009, the government's Board of Investments approved 905 projects worth THB260 billion.

[35] "SBPAC Given Wide Powers," *Bangkok Post*, January 20, 2011, available at <www.bangkokpost.com/news/local/217244/sbpac-given-wide-powers>.

[36] Jason Johnson, "Faint Reform Glimmer in South Thailand," *Asia Times*, November 23, 2010, available at <www.atimes.com/atimes/Southeast_Asia/LK23Ae01.html>.

[37] See, for example, "CRES, Army Seek to Impose ISA," *Bangkok Post*, December 15, 2010.

[38] Muslim Lawyers Association interview.

[39] "Prayuth Apologises to Southerners," *Bangkok Post*, March 21, 2011, available at <www.bangkokpost.com/news/security/228221/prayuth-apologises-to-southerners>.

[40] Bilateral trade is expected to increase between 5 and 10 percent in 2011. Between 2000 and 2010, bilateral trade grew annually by 13.5 percent. In 2010, Malaysian foreign direct investment (FDI) in Thailand hit $95.9 million in five projects, while Thai FDI in Malaysia between 2006 and 2010 totaled $210.48 million. See David Tan, "Plan for Privileged Card to Ease Entrepreneurs with Business Dealings in Southern Thailand," *The Star*, June 3, 2011, available at <http://biz.thestar.com.my/news/story.asp?file=/2011/6/3/business/8827567&sec=business>, and "Malaysia Considers Business Card Proposal to Ease Trade with Thailand," *Bernama.com*, June 2, 2011, available at <www.bernama.com/bernama/v5/newsindex.php?id=590975>.

[41] Don Pathan, "Thailand Refuses Offers from 'Mediators' in the Deep South," *The Nation*, June 15, 2011.

[42] Pheu Thai won 204 constituency seats and 61 party-list seats. The Democrat Party won 115 constituency seats and 44 party-list seats. Bhum Jai Thai won 34 seats (5 and 29, respectively); Chart

Thai Pattana won 19 (4 and 15); Chart Pattana Puea Pandin won 7 (2 and 5); Palung Chon won 7 (1 and 6); Rak Prathet Thai won 4 party-list seats; Matubhum won 1 in each category; and Rak Santi, Maha-chon, and New Democrat parties each won 1 party-list seat.

[43] "Yingluck Pressed on Zone Vow," *Bangkok Post*, July 17, 2011, available at <www.bangkok-post.com/news/local/247391/yingluck-pressed-on-zone-vow>.

[44] Emma Chanlett-Avery, *Thailand: Background and U.S. Relations* (Washington, DC: Congres-sional Research Service, February 8, 2011), available at <www.fas.org/sgp/crs/row/RL32593.pdf>.

About the Author

Dr. Zachary Abuza is Professor of National Security Strategy at the National War College at the National Defense University. He was previously Professor and Chairman of the Department of Political Science and International Relations at Simmons College, Boston. He received his B.A. from Trinity College (1991), and M.A.L.D. (1994) and Ph.D. (1998) from the Fletcher School of Law and Diplomacy, Tufts University. Professor Abuza specializes in security issues and politics in Southeast Asia. He is the author of *Conspiracy of Silence: The Insurgency in Southern Thailand* (2008), *Political Islam and Violence in Indonesia* (2006), *Militant Islam in Southeast Asia* (2003), and *Renovating Politics in Contemporary Vietnam* (2001). He has published two monographs for the National Bureau of Asian Research. His study of the Moro Islamic Liberation Front, which was supported by the U.S. Institute of Peace and the Smith Richardson Foundation, is forthcoming. Dr. Abuza has lectured at the Foreign Service Institute, the Joint Special Operations University, and for the intelligence community. He has twice served as a congressional witness. In 2004–2005, he was a Senior Fellow at the U.S. Institute of Peace, Washington, DC. Dr. Abuza is widely quoted in the press and is a frequent commentator on Southeast Asian affairs in regional and international news organs. He has lived and traveled extensively throughout Southeast Asia.